Military
Vehicles

Jack

SCHOLASTIC INC.

New York Toronto London Auckland
Sydney Mexico City New Delhi Hong Kong

Read more! Do more!

After you have read this book, download your free all-new digital activities.

You can show what a great reader you are!

Military Vehicles
reading fun

enter

For Mac and PC

Do quizzes about the fun facts in this book!

Make a fighter jet
Zoom! Create your own superfast fighter plane.

You will need . . .

Wheee!

Now click the numbers . . .

1 2 3 4 5 6

Enjoy fun activities with simple step-by-step instructions!

Log on to
www.scholastic.com/discovermore/readers
Enter this special code: **L2MVNR6XCC52**

2

Contents

EDUCATIONAL BOARD:
Monique Datta, EdD, Asst. Professor, Rossier School of Education, USC;
Karyn Saxon, PhD, Elementary Curriculum Coordinator, Wayland, MA;
Francie Alexander, Chief Academic Officer, Scholastic Inc.

Distributed in the UK by Scholastic UK Ltd, Westfield Road, Southam,
Warwickshire, England CV47 0RA

ISBN 978 1407 14895 3

12 11 10 9 8 7 6 5 4 3 2 1   14 15 16 17 18 19/0

Printed in the USA   40
First published 2014

Land, air, and sea

Tanks roll across the land. Jets zoom through the skies. Battleships sail the seas. Military vehicles must be tough.

4

Ground force

Land vehicles need to protect
the soldiers inside them. The
Stryker has strong metal armour.
It is fast. It takes soldiers into
battle. Its machine guns fire
back at the enemy.

Stryker

The eight wheels
can speed along
bumpy ground.

This lens helps the crew see at night.

Soldiers can get out of the big door fast!

100 km per hour

Crew: 2

The toughest land vehicle is the tank. This 60-tonne tank, the M1 Abrams, is nicknamed the Beast. It's heavier than six elephants! It has special tracks so that it can travel over rough ground. The soldier on the top fires a gun. This soldier is called the gunner.

M1 Abrams (the Beast)

Tanks through time

Mark 1 🇬🇧
This was the first tank ever used in battle. It was used in World War I (1914–18).

T-34
This tank was used during World War II (1939–45). It had a powerful 76 mm gun.

M48 🇺🇸
This was one of the USA's main battle tanks in the Vietnam War (1954–75).

M1 Abrams 🇺🇸
This is the US Army's main battle tank today.

70 km per hour

 Crew: 4

Boom! The enemy has blown up a bridge. How can tanks get across the river now? Bring in the Wolverine! This tank has its own bridge. It unfolds at the press of a button.

The bridge is ready in just five minutes. It can carry 70 tonnes – the weight of 35 cars!

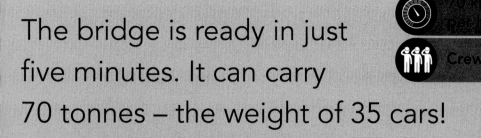

70 km per hour

Crew: 2

The bridge unfolds to be 26 metres long.

Wolverine Heavy Assault Bridge

1

2

3

4

5

The smartest ground vehicle is a robot! BigDog has four legs and can follow orders. It carries food and weapons for soldiers.

BigDog can climb hills and cross rivers. It can travel through snow, sand, and mud. If it is knocked over, BigDog can even get back up on its own.

It's a fact!

BigDog

BigDog can find its own way.

Soldiers use real dogs, too. They can sniff out bombs.

6.5 km per hour

Crew: none!

It never gets lost!

13

In the sky

The military has very special flying machines. Is the Osprey a plane or a helicopter? It is both! It takes off and hovers like a helicopter.

The Osprey can carry 24 soldiers to battle.

Then – *zoom!* In 12 seconds, it becomes a jet plane. It can fly at 465 kilometres per hour. It picks up and drops off soldiers fast.

Osprey

These soldiers are checking one of the rotors. Rotors make the Osprey hover.

NEW WORD

rotor
ROH-tur
A blade that turns to lift a helicopter is called a **rotor**.

SAY IT OUT LOUD

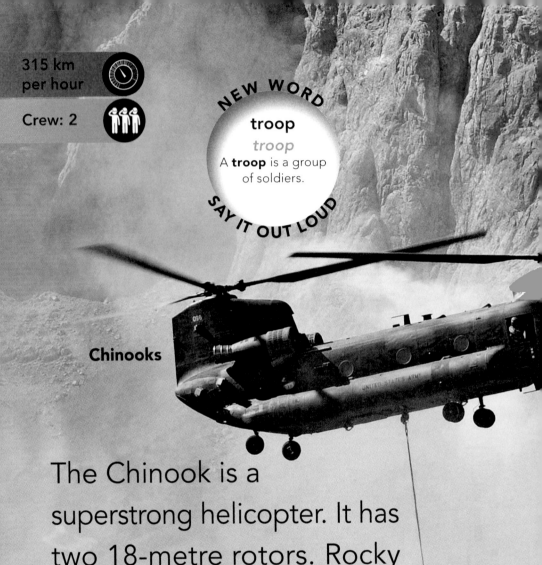

315 km per hour

Crew: 2

NEW WORD

troop

troop

A **troop** is a group of soldiers.

SAY IT OUT LOUD

Chinooks

The Chinook is a superstrong helicopter. It has two 18-metre rotors. Rocky mountainsides. Choppy seas. Hot deserts. The Chinook takes troops and supplies anywhere, day or night.

The Chinook at work

The Chinook is used to deliver supplies. It can carry 11 tonnes.

There is space inside for 55 people, or 2 Land Rovers.

It is strong enough to lift a Jeep. It airlifts injured people.

Shhhh! These are spy planes. The enemy can't see or hear them. But they can see the enemy! They fly high above the ground. Special cameras take pictures of targets far below. Their bombs won't miss.

Stealth bomber

1,010 km per hour

Crew: 2

The stealth bomber flies 15 kilometres above Earth.

Stealth bomber

The stealth bomber's longest single flight lasted 44 hours!

This is the fastest plane ever built.

Blackbird

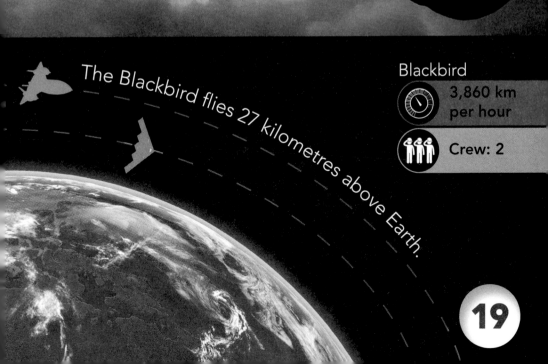

The Blackbird flies 27 kilometres above Earth.

Blackbird

3,860 km per hour

Crew: 2

You can't see me! The F-22 Raptor is invisible to the enemy. The enemy can't see it in the sky.

The Raptor is supersonic. It flies faster than the speed of sound!

F-22 Raptor

Famous fighters
The first fighter jets weren't as fast. But they won a lot of battles!

USA, 1942

NEW WORD

supersonic

soo-pur-SOH-nik

A **supersonic** plane travels faster than the speed of sound.

SAY IT OUT LOUD

2,250 km per hour

Crew: 1

UK, 1944

Germany, 1944

At sea

The navy has a big fleet of battleships. This 173-metre cruiser is one of the first to the front line! It is armed with missiles and guns. Helicopters take off from, and land on, the deck.

55 km per hour

Crew: 400

USS *Princeton*

Dana Scott Canby is a lieutenant in the US Navy. "I love going to sea on ships.... So it's really a dream come true.... You go to sea, drive the ship, manage the weapons systems, and get that sort of experience."

The battleship stands guard. A hovercraft takes troops and supplies back to shore. It rides the waves. It speeds through the surf.

The captain sits in the cockpit.

Air fills the skirt so that it floats.

A cushion of air keeps it afloat. It parks on land. The hovercraft is strong enough to carry a 60-tonne tank!

130 km per hour

Crew: 5

Landing Craft Air Cushion (LCAC) hovercraft

LCAC-02

U.S. NAVY

Fans at the back drive it forwards.

A new US submarine is launched. Some of the crew stand on top and salute. With 12 missiles on board, it is ready for battle.

USS *North Carolina*

50 km per hour

Crew: 143

Important decisions are made in the control room.

Submarines can travel 245 metres below the waves. They can stay there for several months at a time.

Crew members sleep in bunk beds. There are no windows in the bedrooms.

Divers can exit and enter through a hatch.

An aircraft carrier is like a mini-airport. Military planes take off from, and land on, its runway. Lifts move the planes between its decks.

USS *Ronald Reagan*

This carrier is 305 metres long. That's the length of three football fields! The military needs the best vehicles – often big, always powerful.

This aircraft carrier can hold 90 planes.

USS RONALD REAGAN
PEACE THROUGH STRENGTH
CVN 76

Glossary

aircraft carrier
A ship with a large, flat deck where planes and helicopters take off and land.

airlift
To move people or things by plane or helicopter.

army
The part of a country's military that fights on land.

battleship
A ship with many weapons that is used in war.

cockpit
The area in a boat or plane where the captain sits.

crew
A team of people who work together on a vehicle.

cruiser
A large, fast battleship.

fighter jet
A fast plane with guns and other weapons.

fleet
A group of ships.

front line
The place where military forces meet and fight.

hatch
A small opening in a floor, deck, wall, or ceiling.

helicopter
A flying vehicle with large blades on top and no wings. Helicopters can hover and fly straight up and down.

hover
To stay in one place in the air.

hovercraft
A vehicle that moves across the surface of water on a cushion of air.

launch
To set a boat or ship afloat.

lieutenant
An officer in the military.

machine gun
An automatic gun that can fire bullets very quickly.

rotor
The blades that turn and lift a helicopter into the air.

missile
A weapon that is aimed at a faraway target.

navy
The part of a country's military that fights at sea.

submarine
A ship that travels underwater.

supersonic
Travelling at a speed faster than the speed of sound.

tank
A military vehicle covered in heavy armour.

troop
A group of soldiers.

Index

Image credits

Photography and artwork
Alamy Images: 5 tl (Air Collection), 3 bg (James Forte/National Geographic Image Collection), 1 (Mark Hamilton), 14 main, 15 main (Propaganda), 27 bl (RichardBakerScotland), 27 br (Ryan McGinnis), 19 t (Stocktrek Images, Inc.), 9 tl (The Art Archive), 17 t (Tony Hobbs), 18 t, 19 c (trekkerimages); 5 tr, 20 t, 21 t (US Air Force Photo), 16 main, 17 bg (US Army Photo), 29 t inset (US Navy Photo); CombatIndex.com/US Air Force/Airman 1st Class Russell Scalf: 14 inset; DARPA: 12 main, 13 main; Defense Imagery: 15 inset (Cpl. Kyle N. Runnels), 2 t (Gertrud Zach), 8 main, 9 b bg (Staff Sgt. Jacob N. Bailey), 7 tl (TSGT Mike Buytas, USAF); Defense Video Imagery and Distribution Center: 13 t photo (Cpl. Alfred V. Lopez), 10 explosion (Sgt. Ben Brody), 11 b (Staff Sgt. Jason Ragucci); Department of Defense: cover main (Gertrud Zach), 4 t, 6 bg, 7 bg; Dreamstime: inside cover top, 19 r silhouette (Aleksandr Mansurov), 17 br (Corsair262), 10 t bg (Elena Elisseeva), 18 t bg, 19 t bg (Eugenesergeev), inside cover center (Igor Kuzmin), 4 t bg, 5 t bg (Kanate), 10 b bg (Marek Uliasz), 24 bg sky, 25 bg sky (Matthew Collingwood), cover t bg (Robodread), inside cover bottom (Sergey Markov), 18 Earth, 19 Earth (Tomgriger); Getty Images: 2 bl (Barry Iverson/Time & Life Pictures), 32 (Stocktrek Images); iStockphoto: 9 Soviet flag (alfdaur), 23 paper (Electric_Crayon), 6 tire tracks (Jamie Farrant), 8 tire tracks, 9 tire tracks (janraedschelders), speedometer throughout (Kristtaps), people icon throughout (Jeremy), 12 cartoon (memoangeles), 2 arrows (pagadesign), 9 American and British flags (pop_jop), 2 computers (skodonnell), tape throughout (spxChrome), 19 l silhouette (wagnerm25); National Archives and Records Administration/ Department of Defense/Department of the Navy/US Marine Corps: 9 cl; Navy.mil: 26 main, 27 main (Chief Mass Communication Specialist Lucy M. Quinn), 24 t inset (Chief Photographer's Mate Johnny Bivera), 24 main, 25 main (Mass Communication Specialist 2nd Class Terah L. Mollise), 24 b inset, 25 inset; Royal Air Force: 21 bl; Shutterstock, Inc./Paul J Martin: 3 fg; The Image Works/RIA Novosti/РИА Новости: 9 ctl; Tim Loughhead/Precision Illustration: 11 b; US Navy: 30, 31 (Gunnery Sgt. Steven Williams/NAVAIR), 6 inset (Journalist 2nd Class John J. Pistone), 26 b (Mass Communication Specialist 1st Class Jennifer A. Villalovos), 23 b inset (Mass Communication Specialist 3rd Class Kenneth Abbate), 22 main, 23 bg (Mass Communication Specialist 3rd Class Raul Moreno Jr.), 28, 29 bg (Photographers Mate 1st Class James Thierry); US Air Force: 20 b (National Museum of the), 17 bl (Senior Airman Mike Meares), 3 tr (Staff Sgt. Christopher Hubenthal), back cover t, 3 tl, 17 bc, 21 br; US Army: 23 t inset, 29 b inset (Institute of Heraldry), 7 tr, 9 cbl; US Marines: 4 b bg, 5 b (Cpl. Mark W. Stroud), 4 b (Lance Cpl. James Frazer), 10 tank (Sgt. Rachael K. A. Moore), 5 c (Staff Sgt. Matt Epright).